LET'S FIND OUT! *RELIGION*

JUDAISM

MICHAEL HESSEL-MIAL

Britannica®
Educational Publishing

IN ASSOCIATION WITH

ROSEN
EDUCATIONAL SERVICES

Published in 2019 by Britannica Educational Publishing (a trademark of Encyclopædia Britannica, Inc.) in association with The Rosen Publishing Group, Inc.
29 East 21st Street, New York, NY 10010

Distributed exclusively by Rosen Publishing.
To see additional Britannica Educational Publishing titles, go to rosenpublishing.com.

First Edition

Britannica Educational Publishing
J.E. Luebering: Executive Director, Core Editorial
Mary Rose McCudden: Editor, Britannica Student Encyclopedia

Rosen Publishing
Jacob R. Steinberg: Editor
Brian Garvey: Art Director
Nicole Russo-Duca: Series Designer & Book Layout
Cindy Reiman: Photography Manager
Sherri Jackson: Photo Researcher

Library of Congress Cataloging-in-Publication Data

Names: Hessel-Mial, Michael, author.
Title: Judaism / Michael Hessel-Mial.
Description: New York : Britannica Educational Publishing, in Association with Rosen Educational Services, 2019 | Series: Let's find out! religion | Audience: Grades 1–5. | Includes index.
Identifiers: LCCN 2018011029 | ISBN 9781508106876 (library bound) | ISBN 9781508107187 (pbk.) | ISBN 9781508107293 (6 pack)
Subjects: LCSH: Judaism—Juvenile literature.
Classification: LCC BM45 .H457 2018 | DDC 296—dc23
LC record available at https://lccn.loc.gov/2018011029

Manufactured in the United States of America

Photo credits: Cover Oleksiy Maksymenko/All Canada Photos/Getty Images; pp. 4, 21 Culture Club/Hulton Archive /Getty Images; p. 5 David H. Wells/Corbis Documentary/Getty Images; p. 6 Catherine Leblanc/Godong/Corbis Documentary/Getty Images; p. 7 Gemaldegalerie,Staatliche Museen zu Berlin,Germany/Bridgeman Images; pp. 8, 15 ChameleonsEye/Shuttertock.com; p. 9 Naeblys/Shutterstock.com; p. 10 Stevegeer/E+/Getty Images; p. 11 Spiroview Inc/Shutterstock.com; p. 12 Amateur007/Shutterstock.com; p. 13 Menahem Kahana/AFP/Getty Images; p. 14 Blue Green Frog/Shutterstock.com; p. 16 Dave Bartruff/Corbis Documentary/Getty Images; p. 17 David Cooper/Toronto Star /Getty Images; p. 18 Burke/Triolo Productions/The Image Bank/Getty Images; p. 19 Dan Porges/Photolibrary/Getty Images; p. 20 DEA/A. De Gregorio/De Agostini Picture Library/Getty Images; p. 22 © kirill4mula/Fotolia; p. 23 Godong /Universal Images Group/Getty Images; p. 24 Spencer Platt/Getty Images; p. 25 Portland Press Herald/Getty Images; p. 26 © Anne Frank Stichting, Amsterdam; p. 27 Win McNamee/Getty Images; p. 28 GPO/Hulton Archive/Getty Images; p. 29 © Digital Vision/Getty Images; interior pages background © iStockphoto.com/EdwardShtern.

CONTENTS

WHAT IS JUDAISM?

שְׁמַע יִשְׂרָאֵל יהוה אֱלֹהֵינוּ יהוה אֶחָד וְאָהַבְתָּ אֵת
יהוה אֱלֹהֶיךָ בְּכָל לְבָבְךָ וּבְכָל נַפְשְׁךָ וּבְכָל מְאֹדֶךָ וְהָיוּ
הַדְּבָרִים הָאֵלֶּה אֲשֶׁר אָנֹכִי מְצַוְּךָ הַיּוֹם עַל לְבָבֶךָ וְשִׁנַּנְתָּם
לְבָנֶיךָ וְדִבַּרְתָּ בָּם בְּשִׁבְתְּךָ בְּבֵיתֶךָ וּבְלֶכְתְּךָ בַדֶּרֶךְ
וּבְשָׁכְבְּךָ וּבְקוּמֶךָ וּקְשַׁרְתָּם לְאוֹת עַל יָדֶךָ וְהָיוּ לְטֹטָפֹת
בֵּין עֵינֶיךָ וּכְתַבְתָּם עַל מְזוּזוֹת בֵּיתֶךָ וּבִשְׁעָרֶיךָ
וְהָיָה אִם שָׁמֹעַ תִּשְׁמְעוּ אֶל מִצְוֺתַי אֲשֶׁר אָנֹכִי
מְצַוֶּה אֶתְכֶם הַיּוֹם לְאַהֲבָה אֶת יהוה אֱלֹהֵיכֶם וּלְעָבְדוֹ
בְּכָל לְבַבְכֶם וּבְכָל נַפְשְׁכֶם וְנָתַתִּי מְטַר אַרְצְכֶם בְּעִתּוֹ
יוֹרֶה וּמַלְקוֹשׁ וְאָסַפְתָּ דְגָנֶךָ וְתִירֹשְׁךָ וְיִצְהָרֶךָ וְנָתַתִּי
עֵשֶׂב בְּשָׂדְךָ לִבְהֶמְתֶּךָ וְאָכַלְתָּ וְשָׂבָעְתָּ הִשָּׁמְרוּ לָכֶם
פֶּן יִפְתֶּה לְבַבְכֶם וְסַרְתֶּם וַעֲבַדְתֶּם אֱלֹהִים אֲחֵרִים
וְהִשְׁתַּחֲוִיתֶם לָהֶם וְחָרָה אַף יהוה בָּכֶם וְעָצַר אֶת
הַשָּׁמַיִם וְלֹא יִהְיֶה מָטָר וְהָאֲדָמָה לֹא תִתֵּן אֶת יְבוּלָהּ
וַאֲבַדְתֶּם מְהֵרָה מֵעַל הָאָרֶץ הַטֹּבָה אֲשֶׁר יהוה נֹתֵן לָכֶם
וְשַׂמְתֶּם אֶת דְּבָרַי אֵלֶּה עַל לְבַבְכֶם וְעַל נַפְשְׁכֶם וּקְשַׁרְתֶּם
אֹתָם לְאוֹת עַל יֶדְכֶם וְהָיוּ לְטוֹטָפֹת בֵּין עֵינֵיכֶם וְלִמַּדְתֶּם
אֹתָם אֶת בְּנֵיכֶם לְדַבֵּר בָּם בְּשִׁבְתְּךָ בְּבֵיתֶךָ וּבְלֶכְתְּךָ
בַדֶּרֶךְ וּבְשָׁכְבְּךָ וּבְקוּמֶךָ וּכְתַבְתָּם עַל מְזוּזוֹת בֵּיתֶךָ
וּבִשְׁעָרֶיךָ לְמַעַן יִרְבּוּ יְמֵיכֶם וִימֵי בְנֵיכֶם עַל הָאֲדָמָה
אֲשֶׁר נִשְׁבַּע יהוה לַאֲבֹתֵיכֶם לָתֵת לָהֶם כִּימֵי הַשָּׁמַיִם
עַל הָאָרֶץ

Twice a day, Jews around the world say a prayer called the Shema. It starts, "Hear, O Israel, the Lord is our God; the Lord is One." This prayer is an important statement of faith in Judaism, the religion of the Jewish people.

Like Christianity and Islam, Judaism is monotheistic. It teaches that there is only one

The Shema prayer is an important prayer in Judaism. It is recited every morning and evening by observant Jews.

God and that God created the world. Jews believe that God chose them to have a special relationship with him. They must devote themselves to God in all aspects of their lives because God selected them to bring knowledge of him to the rest of the world. They believe that, in return, God has promised to make the Jews a great nation that will eventually draw other nations together in a worldwide community of justice and peace. Today, Judaism has more than fourteen million followers worldwide.

A group of Jewish men pray together in a Jewish house of worship.

Beliefs and Sacred Texts

The sacred book of Judaism is the Hebrew Bible (which Christians call the Old Testament). The first five books of the Hebrew Bible, known as the Torah, are especially important. The Hebrew Bible also contains books of the prophets and collections of poetry, stories, and history. The Torah tells the story of the creation of the world. It also explains and interprets God's laws, including the Ten Commandments. Jews believe that God gave these rules to the prophet Moses.

Copies of the Torah are written on special scrolls that are read aloud during prayer services.

Moses holds up tablets with the Ten Commandments on them in this painting by the Dutch painter Rembrandt.

The Ten Commandments are the most important laws in Judaism. These rules say that there is one God and describe how to treat others. For example, they forbid stealing, killing, or lying. The Ten Commandments also tell Jews to rest on the Sabbath to remember when God rested after creating the world. Jews observe the Sabbath from sunset on Friday to sunset on Saturday. On the Sabbath Jews pray and eat special meals. Work is not allowed.

THINK ABOUT IT
Judaism does not allow people to worship statues or images of God. What are ways to show faith in God that do not involve statues or images of him?

Many Jews study the teachings collected in the Talmud. The Talmud consists of many volumes.

Along with the Ten Commandments, Judaism has other laws. Some laws forbid bad behavior, while others require good deeds. Some laws forbid certain foods, such as pork or shellfish, and explain how foods should be prepared. The Talmud is a collection of ancient Jewish teachings.

COMPARE AND CONTRAST

Judaism has many oral, or unwritten, teachings and customs that Jews follow. How is an unwritten custom different from a written law? How is it similar?

Jewish leaders, called rabbis, wrote down those teachings long ago and added their own stories and comments. The Jewish prayer book, or siddur, contains prayers that Jews recite daily.

In Hebrew, the word Torah means "to teach" or "to show the way." So, in a way, all Jewish teachings—including all of the Hebrew Bible, the Talmud, and other writings—can be considered part of the Torah.

A devout Jewish woman reads from a prayer book, called a siddur in Hebrew.

THE SYNAGOGUE

The Jewish place of worship is called a synagogue. It is the place where a Jewish community gathers to pray and study. A synagogue is sometimes called a temple or a shul, which is a Yiddish word meaning "school."

The leader of a synagogue is called a rabbi, which means "my teacher." A rabbi provides guidance to the Jewish community. Some synagogues also have a cantor. A cantor is a specially trained singer who leads prayer.

The most important part of a synagogue is

This synagogue in Chicago, Illinois, is decorated with the Star of David, a six-pointed figure that symbolizes Judaism.

The Torah scrolls are kept in a special cabinet called an ark.

the ark, or cabinet, that holds the Torah scrolls. A synagogue also has a platform called a bimah, where a reader reads the Torah to worshippers. The main part of synagogue worship is the reading of the Torah. Many synagogues read the entire Torah in one year.

Worship services take place on Friday nights (the beginning of the Sabbath), on Saturday mornings and afternoons, and on Monday and Thursday mornings. Special worship services also take place on holy days and festivals.

COMPARE AND CONTRAST

Different religions have different places of worship and use them for different activities. How are synagogues similar to other places of worship, like a mosque or a church? How are they different?

Major Holidays

The major Jewish holidays fall into two categories: High Holidays and Pilgrim Festivals. The High Holidays are Rosh Hashana and Yom Kippur. Rosh Hashana is the Jewish New Year. The holiday is celebrated in either September or early October. This joyous celebration marks the anniversary of the creation of the world. People gather with family and friends and eat meals with sweet foods, including apples and honey. People go to the synagogue to pray. Prayers include the sounding of the shofar, a trumpet made of a ram's horn. Rosh Hashana begins a ten-day period called the High Holy Days, or the Days of Awe, that ends on

A Jewish man sounds a ceremonial trumpet called a shofar, used in prayers before and during Rosh Hashana.

Yom Kippur. During this period, Jews think about how to live better lives in the year to come.

Yom Kippur is the holiest day in Judaism. This holiday is called the Day of Atonement. It is observed with prayer and fasting. The holiday's purpose is to purify the individual and community. On Yom Kippur, Jews are forgiven for their sins against God. They also ask for forgiveness from people they have hurt. Work is not allowed on Rosh Hashana or Yom Kippur.

Some Jews wear a special white robe on Yom Kippur to symbolize their purity as they ask God for forgiveness.

The Pilgrim Festivals are Passover, Shavuot, and Sukkoth. Passover (or Pesach in Hebrew) celebrates the freedom of Jews from slavery in ancient Egypt. The festival of Passover is one of great joy. It takes place for about one week in March or April. Families eat a special meal called a seder. Before the meal the story of Passover is told. The most important food of the holiday is matzo, which is a flat bread made with only flour and water. This reminds

On Passover Jewish families eat a meal called a seder. Matzo, hardboiled eggs, bitter herbs, and other special foods are eaten.

the Jews of the bread their ancestors, called Israelites, took with them when they fled Egypt for freedom. They did not have time to let it rise because they were in a hurry to leave.

Shavuot commemorates God giving the Torah to the Jewish people. Sukkoth is an autumn festival that observes the time when the Israelites wandered through the desert. Many Jews put up sukkoth (huts or shelters) and pray and eat their meals inside them.

THINK ABOUT IT

Can you think of a special meal or food you eat only at certain times? Why is this meal or food important to you?

A young Jewish girl holds special plants and a fruit called an etrog that are held and shaken during prayers on the holiday of Sukkoth.

OTHER HOLIDAYS

Other Jewish holidays include Purim and Hanukkah. Purim celebrates a time when Jews in ancient Persia (now Iran) escaped a plot to harm them. Purim usually falls in late February or early March. On Purim, Jews go to a synagogue and listen to the story of how Queen Esther convinced the Persian king to stop a plot to kill all the Jews in Persia.

Hanukkah is known as the Festival of Lights. It lasts for

To celebrate Purim, Jewish families have a festive meal, dress in costumes, exchange gifts of food, and give to the poor.

COMPARE AND CONTRAST

Hanukkah happens around the same time of year as Christmas and Kwanzaa. What do these holidays have in common? How are they different?

eight nights and usually occurs in December. Hanukkah commemorates a military victory long ago. In ancient times, foreign leaders took over the Temple in Jerusalem and tried to make the Jews give up their religion. The Jews defeated the foreign rulers and took back the Temple. According to tradition, the Jews only had a small jar of oil for the Temple's lamps. Miraculously, the oil lasted for eight nights. To celebrate the eight nights of Hanukkah, people light candles on a special candle holder called a menorah.

During Hanukkah, Jewish families light candles on a menorah. They also exchange gifts and play games during this holiday.

SPECIAL CEREMONIES

In addition to holidays, there are many ceremonies in Judaism that occur at special times of a person's life, including birth, marriage, coming of age, and death. Shortly after birth, a ceremony takes place in which babies are dedicated to God and named. There is a special ceremony called a bris for male infants. In Judaism, a boy reachesadulthood on his thirteenth birthday, when he accepts responsibility for following the

In Jewish wedding ceremonies the bride and groom stand under a covering called a chuppah.

A Bas or Bar Mitzvah ceremony is often followed by a party to celebrate the occasion.

commandments. This ritual is called a Bar Mitzvah. A boy studies the Torah to prepare for his Bar Mitzvah. During a religious service at the synagogue, the boy reads from the Torah in Hebrew. After the ceremony, many families choose to have a party to celebrate the event with friends and relatives. There is also a similar celebration for girls, called a Bas, or Bat, Mitzvah, which takes place after a girl's twelfth birthday.

COMPARE AND CONTRAST

Do you know of special ceremonies in other religions or cultures that are similar to these Jewish ceremonies? How are they alike? How are they different?

HISTORY

The patriarch Abraham, who lived about 4,000 years ago, is considered the founder of Judaism. According to the Torah, God told Abraham to leave his home and take his family to Canaan (modern Israel). God promised Abraham that they would become a great nation in this new land. This

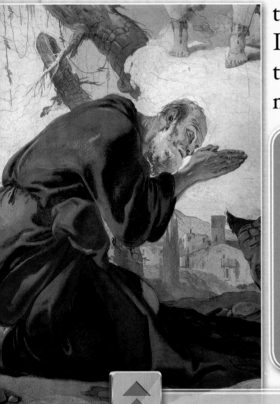

This eighteenth-century painting depicts Abraham, the Jewish patriarch and founder of Judaism whose life story is told in the Torah.

promise is called the covenant.

Long after the days of Abraham, his descendants left Canaan because of a famine and went to Egypt. There, they were turned into slaves. Around 1200 BCE, the prophet Moses led the Israelites out of slavery. God instructed Moses and the Israelites to travel through the desert back to Canaan. Jews believe that God gave Moses the Ten Commandments.

The prophet Moses led the Israelites out of slavery in Egypt. It is told that they crossed the Red Sea as they escaped.

In Canaan, the Israelites started a nation called Israel. Israel became powerful under its first three kings: Saul, David, and Solomon. David made Jerusalem the capital city. David's son, Solomon, built the first Temple of Jerusalem, a center of worship, in the 900s BCE.

THE DIASPORA

In the 6th century BCE, Babylonians destroyed the Temple and took control of Israel. After this, many Israelites left. This was the beginning of the Jewish Diaspora, or the scattering of Jewish people throughout the world. Some Jews later returned to their homeland and

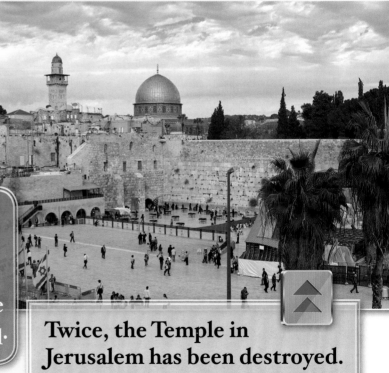

Twice, the Temple in Jerusalem has been destroyed. Today just one wall, called the Western Wall, still stands.

Many Jewish teachings were written down in the Talmud so Jews could observe them wherever they live.

rebuilt the Temple. But the land of Israel continued to be ruled by one foreign power after another. In 70 CE the Romans destroyed the second Temple.

During this time, religious scholars called rabbis became leaders of different Jewish communities. Their teachings were written down so that Jews could follow religious law no matter where they lived. These laws provide guidance on all aspects of life, including food, clothing, business, and prayer.

Over time, the Jewish people spread out to live in many different countries. Today most live in Israel and the United States.

Jewish Movements

In the Diaspora, many different Jewish movements developed. They had different religious, cultural, and political goals. One movement called Kabbala began in the twelfth century CE. Its believers wanted to know God directly by finding secret meanings in the Torah. A rabbi developed a form of Jewish **mysticism** called Hasidism in

VOCABULARY

Mysticism is the experience of spiritual union or direct communication with God.

In the mystical movement called Hasidism, dancing is a way to show closeness to God, to express joy, and to bring people together.

the eighteenth century. Hasidism seeks God in everyday life and places great value on righteous people.

Judaism has three main divisions. Orthodox Jews are the most traditional. They believe that Judaism should be practiced today just as it was in ancient times. In the nineteenth century two groups broke away to make changes. Reform Jews made the most changes. They changed Judaism's laws to make them more modern. Conservative Jews uphold many old traditions but have made some changes in their religious practices.

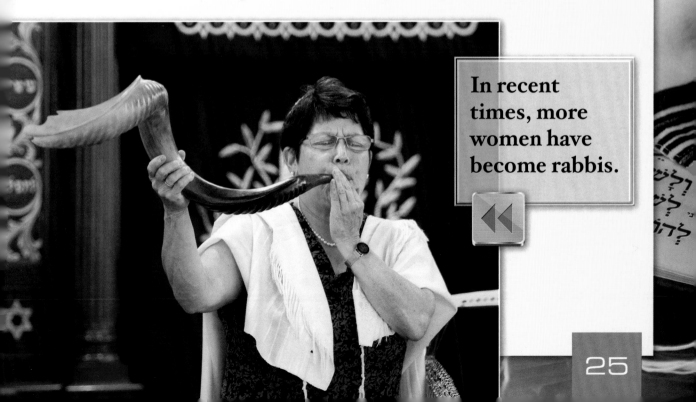

In recent times, more women have become rabbis.

THE HOLOCAUST

When the Jewish people began living in different parts of the world, they were often seen as different. They faced anti-Semitism in many places. This means that people did not like them and treated them badly. Many Jews weren't allowed to have certain jobs or to live in certain places.

In 1933 a leader named Adolf Hitler took control of Germany. Hitler's political party, called the Nazi Party, hated Jewish people. It tried to make life hard for them. Jews could

A young girl named Anne Frank hid with her family for two years before the Nazis captured them. Anne kept a diary that tells part of their story.

A Holocaust survivor lights a memorial candle during a ceremony at the Holocaust Memorial Museum in Washington, DC.

not attend school or own businesses. Later, during World War II, the Nazis decided to kill as many Jews as possible. By the end of the war, in 1945, more than six million Jewish men, women, and children had been killed throughout Europe. This massacre is called the Holocaust.

THINK ABOUT IT

Why is it important to learn about terrible events of the past like the Holocaust?

The Holocaust came to an end when the Allies—the United States, France, Great Britain, and the Soviet Union—defeated Germany. Today, many countries have Holocaust Remembrance days to remember the victims. Many people hope that learning about the Holocaust can prevent such a terrible thing from ever happening again.

MODERN ISRAEL

After World War II many Jewish people wanted a country of their own in their ancient homeland of Israel. This idea is called Zionism. In 1948, the modern country of Israel was created in an area called Palestine.

Many other people had lived in the land for a long time. These people, called Arabs, did not want to give up land that they considered

A Jewish immigrant family sits in their tent at a camp in an Israeli town shortly after the country of Israel was founded.

COMPARE AND CONTRAST

What makes the modern state of Israel different from the ancient kingdom of Israel described in the Hebrew Bible?

theirs. In 1948 the Arabs went to war with Israel. Israel won the war and gained more land from the Arabs. This set the stage for many years of fighting for control of the region.

Today Israel is home to about half the world's Jewish population. It is also home to members of other religions. The country is a modern state based on ancient Jewish traditions.

Tel Aviv is a large multicultural city in Israel and a popular destination for tourists from all over the world.

GLOSSARY

anti-Semitism The hatred of Judaism and Jewish people.

bimah A stand in a synagogue where the Torah is placed.

cantor A trained singer in a synagogue.

commandment An order from God.

commemorate To mark by a ceremony.

Conservative Judaism Judaism as practiced especially among some US Jews that keeps to the Torah and Talmud but makes allowance for some changes suitable for different times and circumstances.

covenant A solemn agreement.

diaspora The spread of a group in different parts of the world.

fasting The practice of not eating for a period of time for religious reasons.

Hebrew The language of the ancient Jews, written in different characters than the English alphabet.

matzo Unleavened bread eaten at Passover.

menorah A holder for candles used in Jewish worship.

Orthodox Judaism Judaism that considers the Torah and Talmud sacred and that strictly follows Jewish laws and traditions in everyday life.

prophet A person who is chosen to bring the word of God to other people

purify To make or become pure.

rabbi A leader of a Jewish community.

Reform Judaism A nineteenth- and twentieth-century development of Judaism in which many older laws and practices were changed or given up to make Judaism more modern

sacred Holy; something important to a particular religion.

siddur A Jewish prayer book.

Talmud The writings that declare Jewish law and tradition.

Yiddish A language related to German that is written in Hebrew characters.

For More Information

Books

Charing, Douglas. *Judaism* (DK Eyewitness Books). New York, NY: DK Publishing, 2016.

DuBois, Jill, Mair Rosh, Josie Elias, and Deborah Nevins. *Israel* (Cultures of the World). 3rd ed. New York, NY: Cavendish Square, 2015.

Klepeis, Alicia. *Israel* (Exploring World Cultures). New York, NY: Cavendish Square Publishing, 2017.

Marsico, Katie. *Judaism* (Global Citizens: World Religions). Ann Arbor, MI: Cherry Lake Publishing, 2017.

McDonough, Yona Z. *What Are the Ten Commandments?* St. Louis, MO: Turtleback Books, 2017.

Websites

Jewish Kids
https://jewishkids.org/

Kiddle
https://kids.kiddle.co/Judaism

National Geographic
https://kids.nationalgeographic.com/explore/countries/israel/

Index